INTROVERT

How to survive, feel more comfortable and socialize better in any situation without social exhaustion

-

Harness your personality, master your psychology & find solitude in an extroverted world

INTROVERT

Text Copyright © 2018 Wallace Foulds

All rights reserved. No part of this guide may be reproduced in any form without permission in writing from the publisher except in the case of brief quotations embodied in critical articles or reviews.

Legal & Disclaimer

The information contained in this book is not designed to replace or take the place of any form of medicine or professional medical advice. The information in this book has been provided for educational and entertainment purposes only.

The information contained in this book has been compiled from sources deemed reliable, and it is accurate to the best of the Author's knowledge; however, the Author cannot guarantee its accuracy and validity and cannot be held liable for any errors or omissions. Changes are periodically made to this book. You must consult your doctor or get professional medical advice before using any of the suggested remedies, techniques, or information in this book.

Upon using the information contained in this book, you agree to hold harmless the Author from and against any damages, costs, and expenses, including any legal fees potentially resulting from the application of any of the information provided by this guide. This disclaimer applies to any damages or injury caused by the use and application, whether directly or indirectly, of any advice or information presented, whether for breach of contract, tort, negligence, personal injury, criminal intent, or under any other cause of action.

You agree to accept all risks of using the information presented inside this book. You need to consult a professional medical practitioner in order to ensure you are both able and healthy enough to participate in this program.

Table of Contents

INTRODUCTION

Introverts and extroverts … they are like yin and yang. First introduced by psychologist Carl G. Jung in 1920, the terms were used to describe what seemed to be polar opposites of the personality type spectrum. In a nutshell, "Introversion means preferring the inner world, thinking about ideas and wanting to understand, while extraversion means preferring the outer world, including people, things and a desire for action," according to Jung. The long and the short of it is that introverts seek to understand, while extroverts seek to act.

While nobody is completely introverted or extroverted, most people tend towards one end or the other of the spectrum. "At the heart of it, introverts and extroverts respond really differently to stimulation," according to the author of <u>Quiet: The Power of Introverts In A World That Can't Stop Talking</u>, Susan Cain in an interview with <u>Huffington Post</u>.

INTROVERT

Extroverts draw energy from stimulation, people and interaction. They are inspired by the world around them and need less alone time to recharge. In fact, their batteries are recharged by external input, rather than internally.

"Introverts feel most alive and energized when they're in environments that are less stimulating - not less intellectually stimulating, but less stuff going on." according to Cain. According to Jung, introverts prefer less external impulses or stimuli, whether it comes from noise, smells, people, etc.

When it comes to understanding something, introverts prefer internal introspection over external, and they turn inwards to process things. They spend time in solitude to mull things over.

Introverts need to be alone to recharge. It's not that they are anti-social, they just need time to regroup after interactions and experiences. In fact, they are probably too busy with their own inner dialogue to engage in social interaction, unless it involves deep conversations about meaningful topics.

Other indications of introversion could be the sense of aloneness even amongst people, the need for downtime, and the reluctance to make small talk. Networking is uncomfortable for introverts, and they prefer to message rather than call.

Jonathan Cheek, Professor of Psychology at Wellesley College, has derived four types of introverts who have different strengths and weaknesses:

Social - Social introverts prefer socialising in small, intimate groups as opposed to large ones.

Reserved - Reserved introverts work at a slower pace because they thoroughly process things before the act.

Thinking - These introverts are introspective and do a lot of self-reflection. They are less averse to social events.

INTROVERT

Anxious - Anxious introverts actually become nervous in situations with too much stimuli and do not have developed social skills. They tend to focus on the negative.

The highly competitive world that we live in today seems to favour extroverts. We are expected to get ahead in social settings, the workplace, even relationships, and oftentimes getting ahead means being heard, being seen, and being remembered. Introverts, to whom these things aren't natural, can be seen to lose out. They feel they need to change like Sandy had to in order to woo Danny in Grease.

How can introverts find a way to hold their own in this world? Here, we will look at how introverts can master any situation, be it social, at college, in the workplace, or in relationships, while staying true to themselves. You will find tips on the best way to handle situations to avoid social exhaustion, and you will discover how to harness your personality, master your personality and conquer the world - in your own space and time.

CHAPTER 1

RECHARGING YOUR BATTERIES - FINDING SOLITUDE IN AN EXTROVERTED WORLD

The world is generally a loud and noisy place, full of stimulation and situations that constantly require us to react or respond. All this drains energy from an introvert, and they generally need more time to recharge after each energy expenditure. Even seemingly simple tasks like running errands might wear us out. Let's look at some good ways to come out fresh and ready to take on the challenges of life in an extroverted world.

I Am Who I Am

Learning to accept who you are and what makes you tick is the key to surviving as an introvert in a world that encourages us to project a certain image. Don't try to be the life of the party if you're not. Don't question what you're comfortable with. Embrace it and make yourself happy doing what you love. You aren't helping anybody, least of all yourself, by pretending to be something that you aren't. Once you show that you are happy with how you are, others will understand and respect that.

It goes deeper than this, however. Ph.D., assistant psychology professor at Davis and Elkins College and author of <u>Introvert Power</u> Laurie Helgoe says that introverts who forgo their true nature actually decentre themselves from their intuition. The further you get from your true state, the faster you will burn out.

Let It Go

The past, that is. It's gone and done with, so there's no point in looking back. You might look back at your younger years and wish you had hung out with that cool group more, or gone to more parties, but remember that that's not what made you tick and you probably wouldn't have been comfortable doing those things anyway.

The Best Policy

Honesty, that is. An introvert really needs to be honest with themselves and other people. Can I really handle taking my parent's overseas friends on a day-long tour of our city? Do I really need to spend 4 hours at my friend's party? If the answer is no, decline gracefully. Expressing your boundaries clearly to yourself and those around you will help you to be the best you can be.

Really take an honest look at what you need to be happy and energised. Only when you're fulfilled can you give your best and have meaningful relationships with others, be they family or that special someone.

The Big WHY

Always go back to the big WHY behind your every action. When this is clear in your head, you can move forward with your energies focussed on your motivation. You can cut out the unnecessary which will drain your energy. The big why will also drive you along when the going gets tough.

Streamline

Once you are honest with yourself, you are able to identify the people, events, tasks and places that tend to suck your energy. Who do you not feel at ease with? What tasks leave you feeling like you need to recharge? Also identify the things that make you feel energized and positive. You can then start to weed out the energy-suckers from your life to make room for more positive pursuits.

Where's The Ceiling?

Introverts aren't adverse to interaction, they just need to put a limit on it. Understand just how much stimulation you can take before you start to get uncomfortable, then call a time-out. Pay attention to your bodily cues, Helgoe advises. "We know at a cellular level when we're losing steam - we may start to feel restless, bored, and even headachy."

Also recognise that you need time to warm up to a person or situation. Give it time, getting to know someone gradually. Be OK with vetoing an impromptu engagement that you weren't mentally prepared for.

My Space, My Time

Create your own little happy space where you can recharge in peace. Decorate it and fill it with things that make you happy. Spend quality time there unwinding and getting into a calm state doing the things that you love, be it writing, drawing or even dancing. Make sure you block out time for this. Don't bring your phone in with you, try to block out any outside distractions and even adjust the lighting to your comfort level.

The Lightbulb

Take advantage of your alone time, since it's when you're alone that you get creative. You will probably feel that your creative juices start to flow during your downtime … make sure you harness them by keeping a notepad or some form of recording device nearby. Aim to record an average of 30 ideas a day so that you don't lose the habit. It's even more crucial to capture those flighty notions since you have nobody else to help you remember them or bounce them off.

Create New Worlds

Introverts generally don't express themselves, preferring to keep their emotions and thoughts to themselves. It's good to find an outlet to express yourself creatively. If you love music, play an instrument or sing during your 'me' time. If you express yourself through art, pursue that in your downtime. Write, if that inspires you, or pursue photography. Get lost in a world that you create for yourself, and you will come out refreshed.

Hobby Horse

Pick up a hobby where you can channel your energy into something productive yet calming. Something like running or hiking is great - you can get healthy and enjoy your solitude at the same time. If others join you, you have the excuse that you're too out of breath to chat!

Creative pursuits are also a great way to channel your energy and learn new things. If you're not too keen on meeting new people and having to be part of a group, don't worry. The activity itself is an excuse to sit quietly and focus your energy on something.

Push It

In accepting that you prefer things to be predictable and at your own pace, it's also good to give yourself a little push every once in a while. Never get too comfortable within your own boundaries that they become walls. Seek out new and adventurous situations in your own way and stretch your horizons. It could be a small thing like talking to an unfamiliar person in a social setting, or a big thing like taking on volunteer work, but these are the things that will grow you into a bigger person.

Keep Good Company

Seeing as how you are more comfortable with a small group of family and friends as opposed to having many acquaintances, encircle yourself with those who tap into the different facets of your personality and enrich your life in different ways. They will accept you for who you are, yet at the same time mould and shape you by challenging you within your comfort levels.

Use your natural inclination towards depth to develop close ties with these people, a closeness and trust that will give you a safe place from which to explore and venture out into the world.

Take a Break

A mini-retreat is essential to an introvert's well-being, so schedule one in every once in a while. Spend one or 2 days away from the normal hustle and bustle of your life; take a weekend away, if you can. Plan to do nothing much during that time, just wander or drive around taking in the sights and sounds around you.

If you can't get away from home, just logging off social media for a couple of days feels like a holiday. You could also work at the park to get some fresh air and a change of scenery. A cute way of breaking from routine is dating yourself for the whole day. Have a picnic, then go watch a movie … all on your own!

Take Care

Take care of me, myself and I. Exercise and eat well. Get outdoors whenever you can and do some form of calming, centring activity like yoga, meditation or qigong.

Take care of others too. Volunteer in something you are passionate about, be it animals, orphans, disaster relief or the elderly. Spreading your love and abundance will remind you of how valuable you are, and get you out of your shell in a productive way.

Self-Improvement

Constantly strive to improve yourself through study, pushing boundaries or facing challenges head-on. Avoid being too critical, but conduct regular self-reflection and really be honest about what you would like to see yourself doing better. It could even be something tangible, like your English, or your cooking skills.

CHAPTER 2

HAVING MEANINGFUL RELATIONSHIPS

1. Kith and Kin

You love your family; they are your life, your love, your joy. You parents, children and relatives - these people are in your life through thick or thin and you love them unconditionally. You would give anything you could to make them happy, and you know they would do the same for you. You have to make their puzzle pieces fit into yours, come what may, but for an introvert, this isn't easy.

The constant demands on you - your mental, spiritual and physical energy will leave you drained if you aren't careful. How do you create meaningful, fulfilling relationships while still taking care of your introverted needs?

- ## **Early Birds Catch the Worm**

Wake up extra early, even if it's only 15 minutes, to spend some time completely free of any distractions or anyone's needs. Do something to boost your energy, be it yoga, a walk, or the first cup of coffee totally on your own. Try to clear your mind of anything for that span of time so as to totally charge up.

- ## **Create Your Own Space**

Carve out a little oasis for yourself. Ideally this would be in your bedroom, but if not, then find a small alcove or the attic or basement. Fit it out with things that make you happy and comfortable, and make sure you spend some time in it every day doing things you enjoy.

If physical space is really not possible, create inner space by blocking out outside stimulation. Put on headphones and retreat into your music. Just remember not to get completely lost in your own world.

▪ Get Out

Take any opportunity to step out for some alone time if you need it. Offer to run errands that need to be done, or just go for a walk. Be gently firm if someone asks to come along, telling them that you need the time alone, but you'll be back with them in good time.

▪ The 2 Letter Word

Sometimes, especially when it comes to family engagements, you just have to draw the line as to how much you can manage before you need to detach and gather your energy. Don't be afraid to say, 'no' and follow it up by explaining why you can't do something at that moment. It's best to express your needs when you're not frazzled, so do it early when your energy hasn't run out. It's also good to explain that your requests for alone time are actually necessary so that you can be your best self.

▪ Share and Care

Whatever you do to protect your inner space, remember that these are people whom you love and who love you. They will respect your need for space, but their need to share in your life and energy is important too, so remember to offer reassurances that you're not deliberately pushing them you just need the time to recharge so that you can be there for them in your full capacity.

▪ Flexibility is Key

In keeping with sharing and caring, remember to be flexible. You may not always be able to have all the time or space you need to fully recharge, but make the best of the time you have and channel whatever energy you have into the people you love.

~*The Best Job in the World*~

Parenting is a full-time job that you get precious few breaks from, especially if your children are still young. Even night time could be taken over, not to mention toilet time, quiet time, work time … You are required to be there for psychical assistance, as well as mental and emotional support. Your whole being is on call for pretty much 24 hours.

Introverted parents are made to feel that they are less than what they should be. They feel that they should savour their every moment with their children and when they don't they feel inadequate and, worse, guilty. Accept that you can only be your best self, even to your children, when you have had time to process, recharge, and renew yourself.

1. Drop the Guilt

Feeling guilty is counter-productive and only drains your precious energy. Just accept how you are wired and work with it. Introversion or extroversion is actually how we are wired, after all, an actual biological nervous setting that we can't change, but only moderate.

2. Compromise

If you're able to, tweak areas of your life to lessen your energy-drain. Cut down on social interactions at work, or do things remotely, like send emails instead of having meetings. Also have a look at your social commitments. You can only spread yourself so thinly, and your priority has to be your children.

3. Their Time, My Time

If you work from home, you will still be invested in your children's goings-on, even if you have Mary Poppins as your nanny. The best thing for both you and your children might be to send them to day-care or nursery where they can carve out their own world away from you. You can then truly have your own time and space.

4. Quiet Time

Family quiet time is crucial to keep things running smoothly in a household. Half an hour of reading or quiet play for your children helps you realign and also teaches your children to appreciate quiet play. Bear in mind that your child might also need these precious recharge moments.

~Handling the Holidays~

Holidays are especially draining for introverts. Relatives and friends all want to see you, you're expected to attend all sorts of social gatherings and, if you have children, they will be home and expecting entertainment. Your children's grandparents might also be expecting to spend some quality time with them, too.

1. Free Babysitting!

Take advantage of the fact that your parents want to spend time with your children ... use them as babysitters! Drop them off for a day of fun and enjoy yourself - introvert style! Recharge, and renew yourself. This goes for any relatives who are willing, too.

2. Care-pool

Don't forget that other parents will also need their alone time, so suggest care-pooling. Take turns to host play dates and organise activities to keep them occupied. They can bake cookies, make decorations, or even watch a movie, and the adults can have their own little gathering or go do what they need to do.

3. Bring Them Along

Do you realise that you have an instant buddy to bring to the myriad of social holiday gatherings? Children will deflect the focus off you, provide you with a talking point, and, when worse comes to worse, you have an excuse to not talk to others … you're tending to your child! You also have an easy escape plan when your child gets restless.

4. I Need My Space

If you have to travel home for the holidays, chances are that you'll be expected to stay at your parents' or relatives' homes. This could be stressful for an introvert - you generally have no space for yourself, and you're constantly expected to smile, be engaged and present at every meal table. Politely insist that you will stay at a hotel where you can have some privacy and peace. If your family really insists you stay with them, compromise by staying for a few nights and then retiring to a hotel. You can lessen the emotional guilt by saying that you want your children to experience something different, perhaps.

5. Cut It Short

Arrange to arrive at a family gathering close to mealtime so that you won't have to drain your energy with long hours of interaction beforehand. If you're staying over, get back to your own place a day ahead, if you can. You'll then have a day to recuperate and regroup before heading back in to work the next day. Even look into cutting your travel time shorter, if possible, by taking a plane or train as opposed to driving. Being out and about means you can't fully recharge in peace.

6. Be a Taskmaster

Prepare jobs for family coming to stay with you so that they will be occupied and less likely to take up your time. Ask the sister who loves to cook to help with the food preparation. The handy brother can help your husband fix things around the house. The children can get busy decorating the place. An added bonus is that introverted guests will also be put at ease with something to do.

2. The Love of Your Life

Relationships are beautiful, but not easy to navigate for any type of personality. There is always the stress of opening up and exposing our vulnerability, only to be left wide open and alone. There is also the fear of the opposite - the risk of becoming lost in someone else, of being engulfed in their life, wants and needs.

The introvert has it even harder - we fear both being engulfed and abandoned at the same time. We have to figure out how to let people in, but at the same time, we are scared that they won't love our real self and that they will push us away. We have to work doubly hard to maintain our own little space while opening it up just enough to let someone else in.

- **Deep Analysis**

Look for the triggers that drain your energy. What situations zap you? Analyse the times you feel you need quiet. What perks you up at those low moments? Also look at which situations take you a longer time to recover from.

INTROVERT

Pay attention to whether you have periods during which your energy levels are higher or lower in general. Does it follow the seasons or the times of the week? All this helps you to pinpoint when and how you can be at your best with your partner, and when you need to be alone.

It is also important to examine how long you need to calm down after an argument. You can then step away from the situation with a clear idea of when you can come back to it to resolve issues.

▪ PDAs ... Yes or No?

Gary Chapman put forward a revolutionary concept in the <u>5 Love Languages</u> that helps us understand the ways in which we most naturally give and take love:

- ✓ Quality Time - time spent together doing fun and meaningful things.

- ✓ Physical Touch - Physical expressions of love and affection.

- ✓ Gifts - Presents, large or small trinkets.

✓ Words of Affirmation - verbal expressions of love, encouragement and acknowledgement.

✓ Acts of Service - things done for your partner that brighten their life and vice versa.

None of these are right or wrong, it's just how we're comfortable expressing our feelings. Accept and work with this, let your partner know, and also understand how they express themselves too, so that you know what works best for both of you.

▪ Communication ... It Works!

You need to communicate your needs and wants. Nobody knows your internal dialogue except you and it's up to you to tell your partner when you need to be left alone to recharge or work through something in your head. Even in a stressful situation - for example after an argument, clear communication as to how much time you need to figure things out in your head will go a long way towards diffusing things.

INTROVERT

Be specific when you communicate your needs. This is to reassure your partner that you really do want to be alone, or that you need fresh air. You might also be able to work out how both of you can get what you want - if your partner wants to get to know his boss better but you don't feel up to getting all dressed up and going to a restaurant, you can suggest they come over for dinner.

This goes for how you give and receive love too. Once you've discovered how you and your partner most comfortably express and receive love, have an open discussion about it. You will then both be more receptive and appreciative of the other's love expressions, which in turn will encourage them to give more of them.

▪ What Are Your Boundaries

Nothing is black and white, and not everything is draining to an introvert. Find out what situations are more bearable or unbearable for you and why. Maybe you don't like going to parties where you don't know anyone, but if it was a gathering of close friends it might be OK. Negotiate within your boundaries, and you will find a middle ground.

▪ Time Is Precious

Quality time - every couple needs it. Figure out how you best want to spend it and communicate that with your partner. To him, quality time might mean partying together, whereas you would be happy just snuggling in bed and reading. Once he understands what would make you happy, you both can enjoy something together.

▪ New Friends

If you are dating an extrovert, they will probably have a large group of friends and they will probably want to hang out with them. You may not feel comfortable in these situations, but since your partner is friends with them, it's unfair to stop them, and equally unfair to force yourself to hang out with them.

Try to go out as a couple and meet new friends with whom you both have something in common. Attend activities you both enjoy and make like-minded friends.

▪ Compromise… A Many Splendored Thing

They say compromise is the key to any relationship, and this is true to an extent. Remember that compromise is a two-way street. It could be the both of you doing something that you're both comfortable with. It could be the two of you doing what your partner wants to do this time, and then what they want to do next time. Or that you both do your own things at some stage. Just make sure that you are both aware of and agreeable to the compromise.

▪ Check In

You've managed to convince your partner to do something calm and quiet with you. Keep in mind, though, that it's not something that they would normally choose to entertain themselves with. Keep checking in on them every once in a while to make sure they are still OK. Keep up a constant flow of communication and your partner will appreciate it.

~*The Dating Scene*~

Dating … the word makes the strongest man quiver, much less the internal-world loving introvert. Put myself out there? Make idle chitchat with someone I don't know? Pretend to be into every little thing they do to try to impress me? Subject myself to intense, personal questions?? No thanks! Take heart with these tips on how to survive a date … and possibly find love! Or at least have a good time.

1. What Works For You

Only you would know what works for you, so focus on what you want and align your energy to have that happen. If 'putting yourself out there' just won't work for you, don't do it. If you're comfortable getting to know someone online, do it for as long as you need to.

2. Profiling

If you're planning on setting up an online dating profile, throw in subtle hints about your introversion. Write about things like your idea of a great date is a quiet, candle-lit dinner, or that your favourite pastime is curling up with a good book.

3. Buddies Breed Buddies

Get to know new people through your friends. That way, you know that they are at least of a similar mindset and you don't have to start from scratch socially with them. You will also have a talking-point in your introducer (discussing their good points, hopefully!)

4. Remember Your Boundaries

Even if you're suddenly Ms or Mr Popularity, don't go date-crazy and line them up for every night of the week. You KNOW that you'll be an exhausted wreck by the end of the week and that it will take a long time to recuperate.

Also remember that if you need to cancel because you truly don't feel up to it, then cancel. There's no point going on a date if your energy is low … you won't have a good time and nor will your date. Offer your date an alternate get-together, and be specific about it so that they won't feel you're blowing them off.

5. Set the Scene

If you set the scene by suggesting what to do or where to go for a date, you'll ensure that you'll at least be comfortable in familiar surroundings, doing things you enjoy and are confident doing and enjoying food that you know and love. With the burden of chartering unfamiliar territory out of the way, you can focus your energy on getting to know your date.

6. Coach, Coach

Give yourself a pep talk before a date, encouraging yourself and running through any eventuality you can think of. Envision what you would do and how you would react in each instant. You will then be more prepared and less flustered.

7. Instant Chemistry?

Connecting with someone is not easy for anybody, and we already know that this is what introverts find difficulty with. Don't expect your very first encounter to be the amazing spark-flying dream of rom-coms. Go in with no expectations and you might have a great time just … having a great time.

8. Where's My Wingman?

Do you feel the pressure of one-on-one dating is too much? Double date! Grab an extroverted friend to be your wingman. They will ease you into the flow of things and smooth over any awkwardness. They can help keep the conversation (and wine) flowing, and you will probably have a better time of it.

9. Front and Centre

Be honest about your introversion with your partner for the evening. This will lessen any chance that they might mistakenly see you as standoffish or uninterested.

10. Reframe

If you're anxious about whether your date will like you reframe the question: are YOU interested in THEM, not the other way around. Looking at it this way takes the edge off it for you - you're not there to impress them, you're just there to have fun and get to know someone.

11. Question Mark

Ask questions about your date that will encourage them to open up about themselves. Think of some quirky or engaging questions that are sure to have you both laughing or chatting away - something along the lines of, "Which famous person you would most like to meet?" or, "If you could choose, what animal would you like to be and why?"

12. Flip It Back

When you're asked a question, return the favour! After you have answered, ask your date the same questions. This will make them feel appreciated and also help you prolong the conversation a little bit.

Be careful how you do this, though. It has to feel natural, otherwise it could lead to awkward moments.

3. Best Buddies

Society seems to think that having a multitude of friends and a full calendar of social activities means you're happy and fulfilled. This may be true for an extrovert, but the exact opposite is true for the introvert. Introverts seek quality over quantity. They don't need that multitude of friends, but of the few friends they do have, they seek depth.

Introverts approach friendship differently, often tending to expect that their friends don't need constant input just like them. It's important to maintain relationships, however, because the old adage of 'out of sight, out of mind' does hold true. You cannot totally be a lone ranger; you need a support group and circle of people with whom you can be totally yourself with. It's also important to make new connections so that you grow as a person.

Keeping In Touch

▪ Ebb And Flow

Do realise and accept that there will always be some hi-and-bye friends in your life, and there will be your true friends for whom you will do anything and vice versa. Also realise that sometimes, in the flow of life, close friends may become distant acquaintances. Don't feel guilty about it. If you want to rekindle the friendship, again, just do it. Take small steps to re-plug into their life.

▪ Pick Up the Phone

Keeping up with your friends, and even your family, will always involve a conscious effort for an introvert. As in anything, small steps towards your goal help to lessen the seemingly insurmountable mountain of calls, texts, gatherings and meet-ups. If you truly want to keep your friendship with someone, just do it! Send a quick WhatsApp, email, Facebook poke, anything to remind them that you're still in their universe. Schedule time to meet and re-connect.

▪ Upon Reconnecting

Don't share all the reasons why you haven't been keeping in touch, nor should you feel you need to come up with reasons. Just be honest and direct, offer a simple apology and offer to try to do better from now on. If the friendship was strong in the beginning, they will understand. If they don't understand, you have to consider that maybe the relationship wasn't so strong to begin with.

▪ Beware The Screen

While it seems that social media is an introvert's answer to keeping in touch, be careful. The casual 'friending', liking or comment every once in a while actually isolates your further from the real connection a friendship needs.

We actually put forth a very distorted image of our lives on social media. Things are constantly out of context - you can post, "I'm feeling down," and all your Facebook friends might send their well-wishes but have no idea as to why.

Conversely, a 'girl's night out' photo might give you the impression that a new friend is a party animal, which will discourage you from deepening the connection because you feel you won't have much in common with them, when in fact it was actually a one-off event for their cousin's

New Connections

- **Friendship Bonus**

If you pursue an activity because you really love it and are passionate about it, you will meet like-minded people. These are the people with whom you might be likely to form lasting bonds with. This works because since you spend a lot of time pursuing this activity, you will be around these people quite a fair bit. This will increase your chances of getting to know them and connecting with them. You will also have a shared passion over which to bond with.

If you seem to enjoy activities where you are predominantly alone, try pursuing them from a different angle. If you enjoy meditation, find a meditation group. Yoga classes are great to learn new poses at. and also connect with like-minded people.

▪ Awkwardness - A Given

Awkwardness is common at most first meetings, especially for introverts. Don't resist this, just go with the flow and once you surpass this hiccup, things will flow more or less smoothly. Resist the temptation to retreat back into your own world just because the small talk is not flowing.

▪ Can You Reach It?

Go for achievable goals when it comes to making friends. Don't expect to find your BFF just because you joined a new painting class ... these things have a modicum of chance and take time. As long as you're making little efforts towards making it happen, you will at least open up opportunities.

Aim to hit a few achievable goals at every event you attend. They could be striking up a conversation with one or two new faces, warmly greeting four familiar faces, or engaging in small talk for at least 5 minutes.

Small Talk - How, Why, What For!?

Small talk - the bane of an introvert's life. More often than not, it's not that introverts don't like to interact, it's more that they prefer a deeper level of connection and a more meaningful interaction. Small talk, to them, is not a good use of their precious energy.

If you flip it around, however, you will find that small talk is actually something that an introvert can excel in and enjoy. You can take control of the conversation and steer it towards something meaningful. Then you can get in, make your mark, and get out while the going is good - remember that quality is more important than quantity.

You are probably not self-indulgent in conversations, so you naturally make your conversation partner feel that they are important by really tuning in to what they say. This is very appreciated in a world where many people don't really listen. Nurture this sense of priority by asking them questions about themselves - even something as everyday "Have you watched (insert new movie title here). What did you think of it?" This is also a good way of not having to contribute as much to the conversation - just let them share.

As an introvert, you are probably more intuitive. You can tap into the feelings and interests of those you are talking to, and use those as cues as to which way to lead, or allow the conversation to flow. Your awareness of your own sensitivities also gives you empathy for other's feelings, so that you know when to change direction or gently go deeper into a topic.

Small talk may turn to generic topics like current events. Make sure you have pre-prepared some talking points about what's going on in the world so that you can contribute to these discussions, or use them to keep a conversation going.

CHAPTER 3

MASTERING COLLEGE

College is an extrovert's dream. You're constantly surrounded by people, noise and activity. You're called on to attend mixers, meetings, clubs, and lectures, and you deal with study groups, discussions and teenage drama. While this is great for those who can handle it, it's a nightmare for introverts who need time and space to process things. Avoid burnout by being smart so that you can enjoy what they call the best time of your life.

Not a Burden

Remind yourself, introversion is OK! It's not a stone around your neck, it's really not. You just need to learn how to manage it amidst the excitement of college and if you can, you'll have a blast like they say you will … just in your own way.

Where to Go?

In the search for a college that suits your introverted nature, consider schools that offer the opportunity for many different socializing styles. Look for those with many various clubs and extra-curricular activities that focus on both academic and social concerns. Go for schools that don't identify themselves with any particular sport or pursuit, like sports or journalism.

While it feels like a small college is the way to go, they do tend to be very insular … everybody knows everybody else and there are very clear-cut cliques. Larger universities are easier to get lost in. They also tend to have more activity options from which you can choose.

Additionally, strong sororities and fraternities offer a sense of community, according to a college administrator. "Introverts who joined sororities did so precisely for the reason that these provide an instant community for those who don't wish to spend tons of time building lots of friendships, because that can be exhausting."

Physically, does the college feel like a place in which introverts would be comfortable? Are there quiet, calm places where you can engage in meditation or yoga? Are there natural oases like ponds, gardens and parks? Are the libraries set up with private study spaces? Does the college designate some dorms to be "quiet zones" where partying is not allowed after specific times?

Keep Close

For your own sanity, consider finding a college near your hometown. Natalie Friedman, NYU Assistant Dean of Students and Director of Learning, Teaching, and Research, Dean of Studies and Senior Class Dean at Barnard, and member of the Vassar English department says, "I see lots of students who cross the country to be at a school they think is "good" because of prestige or location (or because their parents or grandparents went there, but they would be much happier, given their temperaments, being closer to home.

INTROVERT

I knew a student from the west coast [of the States] who came east for school because her mother and grandmother attended the college she was attending. But she was a classic introvert, and also a kid who was sensitive, very close to her mother and siblings, and not very adventurous. She struggled with homesickness, which in turn led her to stay in her room a lot and avoid social interaction with new people. As a result, she didn't enjoy college as much as her mother did, which puzzled her mom. In the end, the student decided to transfer to a school closer to home, and when she made the decision, you could see the relief on her face."

Seek Out The Like

When you are choosing a field of study, consider occupations that are suitable for introverts' sensibilities. Those that are more internally processed or don't really involve people will suit you. You will then enjoy your time studying in relative solitude. Alternatively, choose some electives in these fields.

A Haven to Hide In

Living in unsuitable dorms can be the bane of an introvert's college life. Sharing a space that is supposed to be private is a nightmare with no privacy at all, and a constant barrage of stimulation - your roommates snoring, their typing, the rustle of paper, the whispered conversations ... it will all wear you down. Colleges that offer individual rooms are the better bet, or better yet, your own digs.

First and foremost, your dorm room should be your haven, hopefully yours and yours alone. Try to arrange hang outs at other friends' places or at cafes or the like. That way, you can always retreat to your room for the solitude you need.

Alone, Not Alone

Bear in mind that it's not healthy hiding away in your room all the time, you won't grow as a person. Make it a point to get out, but spend it alone if you want to. Have a meal or walk around the beautiful campus or at the park by yourself every once in a while and you'll be recharged and refreshed for the next basketball game or study group.

Just Do It

It may sound like a contradiction when you're being told to be true to your needs and take time for yourself, but you do have to push yourself to get out there once in a while. Insist on attending sporting events, go to parties and join clubs for things that interest you. College is a time to explore, and if you are smart about it, you'll get the best out of a great experience.

Timing Is Everything

Keeping your sanity amidst the hustle and bustle of campus life takes some strategizing. Arrange to have as many of your classes as possible early in the morning, or late in the evening. You will then be moving about campus during off-peak hours when there is less going on, and you can enjoy the sense of stillness in the atmosphere.

The same goes for mealtimes, which are typically chaotic, noisy and grating on an introvert's nerves. Try eating a little earlier or later than the main crowd and you might be able to grab a few moments of precious solitude.

Nooks and Crannies

The obvious place to look for peace and solitude would be the library, but, as you may be aware, libraries can turn out to be social hotbeds. Explore your campus library and you will discover its "silent spots" where you can camp out.

Venture around the campus and you'll find secluded havens to hide in for your precious alone time. Look for buildings and spaces that are rarely visited and you'll find cherished spaces of solitude amidst the beehive of activity. Take your work or a book there, or even lunch. Be careful, though, and always keep security in mind.

Some campus buildings do feature balconies on some of their floors. These are often deserted, so they offer the perfect hidey-hole for you to squirrel away in. Again, safety should be first, second and third.

Green, Green Everywhere

Most campuses are beautifully dotted with spots of green all around. Ovals or gardens are naturally ... natural and you often feel peaceful when surrounded by nature. The innate sense of expansiveness evokes peace and quiet, making them the perfect place to 'hide'.

Avoid At All Costs

Some places and times of day on campus are just introvert anxiety triggers, so avoid them as if your life depended on it. Lunchtime, when every Tom, Dick and Harry are rushing to be fed and to meet up with their friends, is an introvert no-go. Places like pubs and cafeterias are meant for meeting up and general boisterousness.

It seems that the buildings that house certain fields of study like business or engineering tend to be gathering points for social activity, so steer clear of them if you're not in the mood.

An interesting sociological phenomenon is that at most purposed gatherings, seating is arranged in a semi-circle format, or participants are called upon to form a semi-circle. Similarly, groups are drawn to the semi-circular arrangement. Avoid places where seating is arranged in this format - they will draw crowds. Even look out for this shape in architectural designs ... remember the Roman Coliseum?

The Unavoidable

You're around a lot of people moving here and there ... accidental interaction is unavoidable. What do you do in the lecture hall, for example? Head straight for the back or the sides of the hall so that you will be flanked by the wall. From these vantage points, you comfortably watch the proceedings with less chance of being called upon.

Want to dissuade conversation? Act busy and people will generally leave you alone. Another way to stop small talk in its tracks? Show your not-so-approachable face, but you must obviously use this tactic with caution.

Make your best effort to avoid it, but in the end, you can't totally be a rock or an island ala Simon and Garfunkel, so whenever you do come across a situation, handle it, and then retreat as gracefully as possible.

Gather Your Gang

When you first arrive on campus, take the time to find a few like-minded people with whom you feel comfortable. Just start talking to whoever is around you - in the lecture hall, in the dorm, or sitting next to you in the cafeteria. Slowly develop a friendship with those people you click with. A few quality friends are all you need, not a huge circle of acquaintances.

Innies and Outties

Being amongst like-minded people means you can relax and be yourself without questions and judgement. When you need some quiet time but don't want to be alone, you can count on your innie friends to hang out with you without engaging or interacting in a way that will drain you.

Don't count the outties out, however. They can be your closest friends too, when they understand and respect where you're coming from. They can bring you out of your shell, which you need to do sometimes, to keep things balanced.

Homies

It's not that you don't care as much for them anymore, it's just that you aren't very good at reaching out to people, especially if you have to make the extra effort of calling or emailing. Keep up your ties with your family and friends back home, though. These are the people who have known and loved you for your whole life thus far, and they will always be there for you to retreat to when you just need to BE. No questions asked.

Express Yourself

If you're not ready to speak up in your study group or lecture, but you feel you have something to contribute, request for some time with your professor at their office. You could also email them. Remember that what you have to say is valuable and worth expressing, you just have to find the right moment that you're comfortable with.

DIY

Knitting calms you and gives you a sense of satisfaction? DO it! You don't need to follow other people's idea of fun ...

find something that turns your intellect or creativity on and pursue it. Don't worry if it seems nerdy to others; if you enjoy it, that's all that matters.

~Teaming Up~

We sometimes forget that children also have their own personality traits, but haven't learned to deal with them. Help your child to stay sane in the busy, busy world of school and play-dates where a lot of their time involves being in a team.

1. Charge Up

Little introverts actually need more downtime to process the noisy world. It's doubly important for them because they don't even yet have a full understanding of half of what's going on around them, and how they should deal with it. Remind them to step away from the situation every once in a while - a toilet break or some outside time will perk them right up.

2. The Best Fit

Tell your child to think about what he or she feels comfortable doing and what they feel they are good at.

INTROVERT

Advise them to find a role doing what they are comfortable doing, which for an introvert is generally a behind-the-scenes one.

Most introverts do well at solving problems because they take the time to analyse. They will see tasks through, so follow-up roles suit them, as do detail-oriented tasks. Creative tasks also work for introverts.

3. One by One

An introvert is generally comfortable focusing on one thing at a time - be it a task or talking to people. If your child has ideas to contribute to a group discussion but doesn't want to bring it up to the whole group, tell them to bring it up to just one or two of their teammates and let them help share it with the whole group.

CHAPTER 4

NAVIGATING THE SOCIAL SCENE

Socialising is unavoidable, you will be called upon to attend weddings and parties, go clubbing, and so on and so forth. Small, intimate gatherings where you know and are comfortable with most people are what you're happiest with, but how do you navigate those large bashes where you don't know many people, the noise levels are high and the stimulation could get overwhelming?

Be a Night Owl

Night-time is generally when introverts want to be by themselves to relax and unwind, but it's actually the best time to get out and mingle. This is because we are less stressed at night due to our cortisol levels being at their lowest. When the cortisol levels are low, you are more relaxed and you can handle social situations with a more level head.

A (Wo) man with a Plan

Formulate a plan before attending an event. Work out how you want to play the scene - even down to small details like where you would feel more comfortable standing or sitting, or who you want to target to hang with, if you know these details. Figure out when you want to leave. Even rehearse a little if that helps to ease your anxiety.

The Plan Went Out the Window

For all the advance planning you do, however, always keep in mind that things will change. People who are supposed to be there might not be, you might end up seated at another table, or the party might end up moving to another venue. Anticipate change and you will be more likely to go with the flow.

Tune In, Head Out

Jennifer B. Kahnweiler, PhD and author of <u>The Genius of Opposites</u>, suggests spending some time plugging into yourself before entering a social setting. You can do something proactive like meditate or repeat mantras or just sit quietly for a while. Listening to calm music also works to calm the mind. Close your eyes, take slow, deep breaths and keep still for a while.

The best time to do this is just before hitting the party - in your car or on a bench outside. 10 to 15 minutes should be enough to charge you up.

Hit the Caffeine

According to Cain, coffee or some kind of caffeinated drink boosts your confidence, energy and positivity. She touts, "Coffee will deliver you from self-doubt. It gets you excited about new ideas and helps you ignore the chorus of judgers inside your head. It propels your thinking and helps you make connections between seemingly unrelated things. Hence, the saying that 'a mathematician is a device for turning coffee into theorems.' "

Have a cup of coffee or some other caffeinated drink about half an hour before going to an event. Coffee takes about 45 minutes to be absorbed into your system, and lasts around 4 to 6 hours, so have another hit of caffeine around 2 hours into the event if you think you will be called upon to stay for longer than 4 hours.

Bring a Friend

An extroverted friend, that is. Chances are, many of your friends are extroverts, since opposites attract to balance each other out. Your extroverted friend could be your key to comfort in a social gathering, especially if you don't know many people there. Helgoe says, "They'll understand you may not want to talk to everyone and can help introduce you to people you'd like to connect with."

Your extroverted friend can also help to talk you up, and, when the time comes, will understand your time out cues. They can then help you to negotiate your social limits smoothly.

Hey Buddy!

Act like everybody is already your friend, even if you're just meeting them for the first time. Greet them warmly, ask about their work or family, or enquire about life in general. Don't forget to share about yourself too!

Team Up

If you aren't able to bring a friend to an event, look around the room for other introverts who seem to need help joining in. You might be more comfortable talking to them since they will probably understand your awkwardness and respect your need for conversation gaps. Team up and take turns striking up conversations with others, lessening your chance of social burnout.

Stand Tall

Fake it 'til you make it, touts John Zelenski, Ph.D., psychology associate professor at Carlton University. If you normally feel small, stand tall. If you are nervous about voicing out your opinion, voice it out louder. If you avoid interaction, make conscious eye contact. Keep being the person you want to be by doing what they would do until you believe that you are that person.

Confident poses like straightening your spine, spreading your legs and putting your hands on your hips actually boost your cortisol and testosterone levels, which boosts your confidence, according to social psychologist Amy Cuddy.

Laughter is the Best

You may be dwelling in your inner world, but you can reassure others around you that you aren't standoffish by offering a simple smile or direct eye contact.

A smile is seen as an extroverted trait. It makes us seem more upbeat, social and approachable. Charles Darwin himself examined the science of smiling in his book <u>The Expression of the Emotions in Man and Animals</u>. It's not understood why, but the simple smile sparks off physical and emotional positivity in both the giver and the receiver, giving an instant high. Use its silent power to your advantage. "A smile is the shortest distance between two people," according to entertainer Victor Borge.

A genuine laugh when something funny arises shows that although you're not a clown by nature, you do still appreciate humour and that you are … human.

Get Out of Your Head

Introverts are generally happier conducting their own inner dialogue than engaging in idle chit-chat with others, but in order to be truly happy, you cannot hide away in your own head forever. You have to find a comfortable balance between maintaining your own space and interacting with the outside world. In a social setting, make a conscious effort to get out of your head for a little while and continue conversations you might normally cut short. If you don't want to contribute too much, you can use your listening skills to encourage the other person to talk more. You may learn or gain something in the process.

One Mouth, Two Ears

You know the famous saying ... we are all given one mouth and two ears, so use them accordingly. Introverts are naturally better listeners. We are not impatient to push our point and we really pay attention to what is being said, as well as the context in which it is being said. This includes reading between the lines and body language. We also carefully analyse things before we take action. These traits are all advantages in relationships in general. They allow you to build relationships that are deeper and stronger. Leverage them smartly!

Bear in mind that you are extra-sensitive to external stimuli. If you feel you have to focus all your attention on what's being said, try to minimise outside distraction. Request to go to a quiet place. The person you are focussing your attention on will feel and appreciate your sole focus and total presence.

Do Your Homework or Play Detective

Small talk - you have to do it. Kahnweiler touts doing your homework before attending an event. If you can, gather a little intel about some of the people who will be there. Formulate some questions and comments that you can use as conversation starters or fillers.

If you really don't know anything about the people attending the event, formulate general questions based on the event. If it is a school event, ask, "How many children do you have?". You can also bring up something personal, for example, if you've just come back from a cruise, share your experiences, good or bad. If you are at a total loss, listen in on conversations and pitch in when you can.

Buy Time

Kahnweiler says, "A lot of introverts can become anxious about what they should say next in a conversation - so much so that they miss what the other person is saying." You can fill a gap in the conversation by rephrasing what was just said in your own words. This will show that you're listening and processing what's being said, and buy you time to respond.

Press Repeat and Deflect

Develop a set of answers to questions that you probably will have to field, especially if you are attending a family function or a social function where you've not seen some people for a while. You might have to answer questions like, "When are you settling down?" or, "Do you have someone special?" repeatedly throughout the function, so giving automated answers will save you the brain-drain of coming up with clever, yet non-committal ones.

Also practice gently deflecting when the conversation leads to topics that you aren't comfortable discussing, like politics.

Work It

Taking on a job eases the anxiety of being in a crowd. Busy yourself in any way possible, from bussing tables to handing out drinks or taking care of the children. When you are occupied, you won't feel as stressed nor awkward standing alone, and you will be less likely to be imposed upon to make small talk or. You might also find like-minded people as you are going about your business, and this might lead to the more meaningful conversations that introverts prefer.

Shutdown Time

Understand and accept that you will have moments of shutdown when you just need to get away from the crowd, the noise, the conversations and the hustle and bustle. When you feel like you are fading out, slow your breath down and excuse yourself for a while. Helgoe suggests, "try being very still, as if you are waiting for the other to finish, then looking down or away, which can communicate you're ready to move on." You can wait for a pause in the conversation and make your excuses.

Get some solitude by going to the bathroom, out to the balcony, or even pretend to make a call. Ten minutes of reconsolidation should get you back onto your social feet.

Also recognise that you have your social limits whereby enough is enough. For some introverts, one or 2 hours is really all they can take before they have to make their excuses and go home. Maximise the time you have at an event. Talk to the people you really want to, do the necessary, and get out while the going is good.

~Connect~

Making connections is one of the things that introverts need to make a conscious effort to achieve. Whether in the social domain, relationships, or at school or the workplace, you won't get anywhere without the ability to connect with people, and you need strong connections with people who will support you and help you to be the best that you can be.

You never know who will make an impact on your life - it could be the love of your life, a casual acquaintance, a customer or a boss. So push through the mental barrier and never stop making connections.

1. One

Remember that we are all actually already connected; just different parts of one big whole. This sounds like a hippie-dippy thing to say, but if you think about it, it's true. We came from the same beginnings (the Big Bang, Creation, whatever you believe in). We all have trials and tribulations, great joy and great tragedy. We all are a part of Mother Nature. We all have similar body structures. All we need to do is take that one step further to make that mental and/or emotional connection. Blaz Kos, personal development author, life strategist, personal coach, start-up enthusiast and online entrepreneur reminds us,

"You don't see the connection? Very simply: if you litter the Earth, everybody is exposed to the damage. If you make a few people happy and they make a few people happy, you can make a whole nation happy, and several happy nations can mean a happier planet."

2. What Ice?

Coming from the standpoint that there never was any ice to begin with, gets you a long way towards not having to deal with it. If small talk really isn't your thing, skip it. You'll actually make a better first impression this way - showing that you're comfortable enough to not feel the need for preliminaries.

Skipping the small talk also means that you can immediately start searching for a way to build a bond. Conversely, if you really can't find common ground, you can bow out graciously without having spent too much time on it.

3. Create Awesomeness

Do things that are so mind-blastingly awesome that your reputation will precede you. People will then want to make the connection with you, and they will be the ones approaching you, rather than the other way around.

CHAPTER 5

GETTING AHEAD IN THE WORKPLACE

Introverts work better when they have the time and space to work and think on their own. They generally need order and peace in which to be creative. When it comes to projects and meetings, introverts prefer small groups and projects that highlight each individual's talent, and they are more comfortable getting their message across in writing.

The problem is that the workplace is generally not a conducive place for an introvert. The office setup often leaves no room for solitude and there are constant stimulations, interactions and demands, all of which suck energy and slow productivity, according to Cain in an interview with Harvard Business Review. She references a study in which introverts and extroverts were given math problems to solve while background noise was played. The volume of the background noise was turned up and down at various intervals throughout the study, and researchers found that introverts were at their most productive when the noise level was lower, whereas the opposite was true with the extroverts.

An introvert can hold their own in the fast-paced workplace if they work smart and stay true to themselves. Cain emphasizes, "We know that introverts are very creative because their very propensity for working in solitude and with a lot of focus actually aids in the creative process. When psychologists have looked at who have been the most creative people over time in a wide variety of fields, almost all the people they looked at had serious streaks of introversion, They were comfortable going off by themselves and focusing."

Turn the Camera In

Do some self-reflection and examine the positions you've held in the past to highlight your skill set, as well as your faults. Objectively analyse both, and you'll have a clearer picture of what you are capable of. Even look into your hobbies to see what really makes you tick.

That said, recognise that introverts have traits that contribute greatly to the workplace. Cain says, "Introverts are persistent, diligent, and focused. [They will solve a difficult problem], and they'll work harder and longer than extroverts."

There is also a creative advantage for introverts, according to Cain. "A crucial part of being creative is being able to go off by yourself and think things through."

Choose Wisely

"Finding roles that fit your needs," Cain advises, is one of the important keys to coming out on top in the workplace. Since you aren't comfortable with large amounts of interaction and need a longer time to process it, find a type of work that allows you to be more solitary.

INTROVERT

In this day and age, the concept of 'work' has become a lot more flexible and you can tweak many careers to fit your personality and comfort level. Even a job like human resources, where you are typically required to interact with many people throughout the day, can be tweaked to suit an introvert's personality.

Location, Location, Location

It goes without saying that where you spend most of your day will affect your happiness and productivity. Many companies are much more sensitive to our emotional needs nowadays, and you generally aren't stuck with what you're given, work-wise or in terms of office space. Negotiate a way in which you can be productive in an environment that is comfortable for you, be it a corner cubicle that's a bit more shielded, or even at home, at your computer.

If more secluded permanent office-space isn't available, look for a spot where you can have a few moments of solitude every once in a while. You will return to your desk refreshed and charged up.

Take It in Batches

Do similar tasks in batches, like finishing all your administrative work in the morning, then shift your energy onto other things that can be batched together. Introverts focus intensely on something, so they need a longer time to refocus their energy. By batching, you will up your productivity at each task you do and you won't frazzle your brain.

The Sky Is Not the Limit

An introvert has to tap into their mental health as well as their physical health to stay on top. We know what's good for our bodies, but we often think we can power through with multiple meetings throughout the day without a thought as to our mental limit.

Take note of how many team projects you can attend before you start to get frazzled. You can only handle so many before you need to sit down and sort through it all to get a handle on what needs to be done. Take a leaf from the pages of LinkedIn CEO Jeff Weiner. He makes sure he spaces out his meetings throughout the week so that he has time every day to process what was discussed and what needs to be done to move forward.

Listen To Your Intuition

Be in tune with your intuition … it will generally steer you away from unnecessary things that will overwhelm you. Remember the 80/20 rule of productivity in which 80% of the results we churn out are created by 20% of the work we do. Listening to your intuition will guide you away from the unproductive so that you can spend your precious energy on the work that will get the results.

Go It Alone

Get organised and go it alone. You have a great capacity to explode with creativity and insight when you are allowed to go deep into yourself, but you are very easily distracted by any stimuli that intrudes. Do these things to allow yourself to focus:

- ✓ Distinguish between the urgent, the important and the trivial. Consciously focus solely on the urgent first.

✓ Cut out all distractions. Be very serious about this, as you know that any small distraction throws you off your game. Even your own mind can lead you astray - as can a mote of dust in the sunlight … a line of your favourite song…

✓ Develop a productivity system where you focus on one task at a time, and stick to it at all costs. Include things like writing down ideas and tasks to complete.

✓ Snap yourself back to the task at hand by constantly referring to these tools.

✓ Allow a certain time for daydreams, then consciously put them on the backburner.

The Right Team

While introverts generally shy away from too much interaction, they can work well in teams thanks to their intense focus and ability to pinpoint the diamond point amidst the myriad of input, given the space to focus.

INTROVERT

If you have to work with a team, try to arrange it such that each team member has a role to perform towards the final goal. For an introvert, this is preferable to a team that operates on group planning, brainstorming and decision-making.

Introverted lab assistant Taylor Curley shares that he prefers 'cerebral jobs' for which he and his teammates have to solve complex problems on their own, only collaborating when they have had time to process things for themselves.

Recharge

It's been said time and time again, but that's because it's true. Recharging is the key to an introvert's success, in anything they do. This is especially true at the office where a positive and calm mind-set leads to high productivity. Don't worry, "renewal is not for slackers," CEO of The Energy Project Tony Schwartz reassures.

If we look at our office surroundings, we realise that we are surrounded by a high level of digital energy, which is draining on the most extroverted of us. Introverts, need to step away from this draining energy flow. Schwartz advises in a <u>Huffington Post</u> interview, "We're trying to keep up with our technology - the digital flow operates at this very high speed continuously. Whereas we're designed to operate rhythmically, to move between activity and rest; that's when we're at our best." So taking a physical break from this charged atmosphere, as well as from the chatter and bustle. Take lunch outside, or just go for a walk, if possible.

Check In

Introverts would be more than willing to isolate themselves and focus on their work hour after hour. Cain says, however, "We all know that part of doing a good job is forming the bonds, connections and relationships that we all need."

Make it a point to take a walk around the office every day, stopping to chat with colleagues. At first, you will feel like this is a chore, but in time it will begin to be a natural thing. Ignore the niggling sense that you're wasting your time. Cain insists that "scheduling in a half hour or 45 minutes a day to do that can go a long way."

It's especially important that you make the effort to regularly check in with your superiors and team members. Do this before they check in with you and they will praise your initiative.

Medium Should Equal Message

Although you're more comfortable shooting out emails from behind your desk, realise that this may not always be the best medium to pass the intended message through. For one thing, keep in mind that people may not check their emails as often as you do. Additionally, if it's a fairly urgent message, you might want to text them, call them, or just find the person directly.

Some interactions just need to be face-to-face, so be sensitive to this. I watched a movie in which the main character was a freelance downsizing agent. He navigated this sensitive minefield with as much warmth and encouragement as he could, and most employees came away from the meeting … well, at least not gutted. A plan was put in place to 'modernize' the whole operation, and deliver the message via screen-chats. You can imagine the disaster that ensued.

Finally, half of work-life relies on the relationships you form with your co-workers and superiors. Relationships can only be formed in person.

Social Media

There is a place for social media in the workplace, however, so don't discount it. Use a social media site to pave your way to a smooth meeting by introducing yourself and offering a little profile so that others can get to know you a little without the requisite small talk that precedes many gatherings. You can also forward some highlights of what will be covered at meetings, as well as touching base with clients with whom you've not been in touch with for a while.

Some introverts tend to work better with the written word. If you are one of them, leverage this strength. According to Koz:

"In the digital age, you have numerous options for how you can take advantage of the ability to communicate well in writing as an introvert. You can write articles on platforms like Medium, do guest blogging, start your own blog, post slides on SlideShare or answer questions on Quora. Today, you can build your own brand as an introvert by producing lots of quality content on different media platforms."

Game Plan

Always, always, always have a game plan before going in for meetings or discussions. Being prepared means that you won't feel the pressure of bringing up important points at the drop of a dime, and it will also ensure that you have valuable contributions to make to the proceedings. Try to find out the main points of the meeting, and even what other attendees will bring up so you can plan your contributions ahead of time.

Speak Up

Introverts generally speak softly, but in a meeting, especially if it's a conference call, you have to make a conscious effort to project your voice. Your tone of voice also makes an impact. Take care to speak at a measured pace. Speak clearly and articulate in a natural way.

A strategy to inject yourself into the proceedings is to make your first contribution within the first 5 minutes of a

It could just be a remark or question, but it will ensure that others will see you as present and contributing.

As an introvert, you probably don't speak up too much, so make sure that what you do say is meaningful and impactful. You are probably quite adept at analysing the situation, so take your time to do so and come up with something that makes more sense than what has already been said. You can also offer a concise summary of all that's been said, offering the diamond point on a platter which works brilliantly when the meeting is going off-track as meetings sometimes do.

You can also hold your own against the more verbose in the group. If you have something to add, you can put your hand up and gently interject with something like, "May I say something here."

Idea (Wo) Man

If you've been keeping a note of all the wonderful ideas that come to you during your quiet introspection time, make use of the fact that you are good at analysing, prioritising and making connections, as well as developing a game plan to bring the great ideas to fruition.

- ✓ Share your ideas with your boss, your supervisor, or your business partners. Even share them with your friends and family since you never know who might be able to help you grow your ideas and bring them to fruition.

- ✓ Consider sharing your ideas online by publishing presentations and articles, writing blogs or answering questions and participating in discussions.

- ✓ Actually plan a course of action to bring your ideas to fruition.

- ✓ Hit execute and DO it!

The Diamond Point

Concentration is another great attribute that introverts can be proud of. You have the ability to process a lot of information and dig out the diamond points. You can then use these diamond points to make creative connections and formulate informed courses of action.

This attention to detail gives you an edge as the devil is in the details, as they say. You can see what others may have missed. You have a larger impact when you do put in your two cents worth, and you are able to handle risks better.

What should you do with this trait?

- ✓ Master and leverage technology to your advantage.

- ✓ Develop a high-grade system to harness, process and connect information.

- ✓ Grow your knowledge, become an expert, and ensure that you are known as one.

- ✓ Push your concentration powers by tackling large, complex tasks.

INTROVERT

- ✓ Search for small but crucial details that have been missed by your peers.

~Top 10 Careers for the Introvert~

Here is a short-cut to narrowing down what careers would typically allow you to work more or less on your own. Obviously, you can't be completely cloistered away for the whole duration of your work day, but at least the nature of the jobs featured here allows you to fly mostly solo.

1. Writer

Writers produce the written word for ... mostly anything. They work mostly behind their computer screen at their desk - a happy place for an introvert. Even interviews and job assignments can be done via email or, at the very least, via online chats.

2. Archivist

What does an archivist do? They care for and keep important documents. They catalogue, write descriptions for, and systematically file them away.

Archiving is a solo man's work unless you organise or collaborate on lectures and workshops featuring the collections you're responsible for.

3. Lab Technician/Forensic Scientist

As a lab technician or forensic scientist, you process samples in a lab. Your workmates might be fellow technicians or scientists, but you mostly work alone at your station. The only time you might be called upon to interact is if you have to present your findings in a briefing.

4. Pharmacist

The pharmacist fills out prescriptions and doles out medications to customers. There is higher exposure to interaction with customers, as part of the pharmacist's job is to explain how to use the medications they dole out. You can limit this by working in a pharmacy that doesn't need you to be at the front desk the whole time, rather you can be on call. You could also work in a hospital, completely in the background filling the prescriptions out while someone else deals with the patients.

5. Translator

A translator of written material, that is. Your job is to basically translate documents from one language to another. You're ensconced behind your computer screen and you even receive and submit your work online, so interaction is very limited.

6. Graphic Designer

Graphic designers work with visual images to get messages across. Aside from the briefings and presentations, they are lone rangers, coming up with their designs alone. If you are self-employed as graphic designers are at the liberty to be, you can really work from a happily isolated space.

7. Computer Programmer

A programmer truly lives in their own little world, inputting and developing the code that makes computers tick. They interact predominantly with the screen when they are doing the actual coding, which is most of the time. There are interpersonal demands on the programmer, however. You are generally required to work in a team to apply the coding.

8. Archaeologist

Research and exploration are what archaeologists do most of the time. They are detectives who uncover clues into past civilizations by excavating ruins, collecting artefacts, and examining them. They then write up their findings.

Most of this is done in solitude, and the only time you would be called upon to interact with others is when you present your findings with your peers or collaborate or consult on projects.

9. Photographer

Photographers take pictures that tell stories. Most of their interaction is when they have to talk to their subjects, which is avoidable if the subjects are objects. Another aspect of the job is editing images, which can be done alone. Be aware, however, that the photographer might have to travel around to shoots and events, so if you prefer to stay close to home, take this into consideration.

10. Geoscientist

As a geoscientist, you examine the earth's structure and composition. You spend most of your days searching for natural resources like petroleum, metals and groundwater. As a scientific study, geoscience requires you to use your critical thinking skills to come up with solutions, something which an introvert excels in. You indulge in a lot of research and analysis. You are also not required to interact much in your day-to-day work.

~Interview!? Keep Your Cool!~

Do you break out in a cold sweat at the mention of putting yourself out there? Interviews are doubly nerve-wracking since you have to present your best self to get a job. What if the interviewer doesn't understand your lack of verbal generosity isn't reticence, you're just careful with your words? There are ways to put your best self out there to impress your way to the job you want!

1. Strategize

An introvert must strategize to make sure they're always at their best at each interview. If you are interviewing more than once in a day, keep a buffer time in between each interview to re-gather your energy.

Make sure you have enough time … half an hour might just do the trick, but if you're really lucky you can plan your first interview at the earliest time possible when you're energy reserve is full, then your next one after lunch, perhaps. If that's not possible, plug in some headphones and try to have a quiet coffee somewhere outside.

Being sure of the exact location of the interview is also crucial to how you will perform. You don't want to be rushing in last-minute, all flustered and messy.

2. You vs a Panel

If you are faced with a panel of interviewers, you will likely be thrown even more off-keel since, as an introvert, you are more comfortable with a one-on-one meeting. Gather yourself and see them as all parts of a whole.

When you are introducing yourself, either shake hands or at least make eye contact with each panel member. During the interview, address as many of the panel as you can.

3. Small Talk

In an interview, small talk is a way for your employer to gauge a few things like how comfortable you are around people and if you're able to adapt and go with the flow, not to mention how intelligent you are. If you have a chance, initiate the small talk with a few pre-prepared conversation starters. Ask purposeful questions like which restaurants nearby the office block does your interview enjoy? Aside from putting your best foot forward, small talk helps you make a connection with your interviewer.

4. Begin and End on a Strong Note

First impressions are real, pay attention to how you come across as soon as you walk in. This is actually good for the introvert. Stride in confidently with an enthusiastic greeting. Even before your initial handshake, make a comment about your journey, the weather, your surroundings, anything you can think of. Make your handshake a firm, confident one, and your interviewer will already have decided that you're confident, outgoing and enthusiastic. Even if your energy wanes halfway through the interview, this initial impression is still powerful enough to cover for you.

Round up the interview in the same way, with a bang. Give another hearty handshake and big smile and say something along the lines of, "Thank you for your time, and for the opportunity!" Interviewers will generally review the interview straight after it's done, so the last impression you leave will linger and be locked in.

5. Match Them

Use your observational ability to observe the people in the room - the energy and emotional status of each person. Follow the mood that each interviewer is setting, as much as you can. In this way, even if your energy is waning in the middle of the interview, you can still maintain an illusion. Additionally, introverts may seem standoffish and uninterested just because they process things internally before responding. Avoid giving your interviewer the wrong impression by emulating their tone and pace.

If your interviewer is keeping things light and casual, follow suit. If they are professional, you should be too. If the energy is high, raise up your energy to that level. Even pick up some of their body language since half of what's being said is said through gestures and facial expressions. Just be careful to tread lightly and not overdo it.

6. Play up the Positives

Make it a point to upsell your positive points, some of them due to the very fact that you ARE an introvert. Show your interviewer that you are thoughtful, thorough, considering, and engaged. Emphasis to them that you will see something through in detail and give deep analyses to things before acting on them.

If you feel that upselling your achievements is too much like bragging, put them in the context of what you learned from them, and how they can benefit the company you're interviewing for.

7. Admit It

You never know, your interviewer might be an internal energy recharger too! If you bring it up, it could go a long way towards your interviewer understanding where you are coming from, and finding you an appropriate fit.

Make sure you bring up the positives about your nature. Play up your strengths. The reply to an enquiry into your strengths could be, "Due to my introverted nature, I naturally listen, observe and analyse before I go ahead with something. This makes me more informed and focused on my next plan of action."

Another common interview question is, "What are the aspects of your work style that you would like to work on?" Be honest! "I do find that I am more comfortable emailing than speaking on the phone or face-to-face. While emailing is efficient and you end up with a good record of what was discussed, I do realise the interpersonal benefits of a face-to-face discussion, so I am working towards in-person meetings, followed up by a summarizing email."

~Working the Network~

If you're a freelancer, you're bound to have to network to grow your business. Even if you're very good at what you do, you need to get the word out or nobody will be aware of it. How can an introvert, to whom networking is not natural, get ahead in this game?

Networking is basically socialising with a purpose, so you can use many of the same techniques that you use to conquer a party to build your business contacts. These include using your extrovert friends to up-talk you and smoothen your way during events, making and sticking to a plan, and faking it until you make it.

1. Practice Makes Perfect

Much as personal networking is draining and to be minimised, it IS important. The best way to make it easier is to simply practise until it feels natural. Start off with short stints, initially; plan to attend a networking event for 1 hour, and even plan how long you want your conversations with each target to last. Gradually increase your exposure until you hit your absolute limit.

2. Line 'Em Up (Your Ducks)

Make a plan of who you wish to target at networking events, and what you want to talk to them about. Stick to the plan and you won't feel lost at sea when in the thick of the action.

Also prepare yourself physically. Put on a comfortable outfit, wear your hair in a way that you're comfortable with, yet suitable for the occasion, and prepare all the materials you'll need in an organised manner so that they'll be at your fingertips when you need them. This way, you won't be flustered or uncomfortable in an already nerve-wracking situation.

3. Be an Early Bird

Part of your pre-game plan should be to arrive at a networking event early. This way, you can familiarise yourself with the lay of the land or strategize as to where you want to position yourself, and so on. You can also spend some time to ground yourself before the crowd arrives.

Take this a step further by making a connection with some people you know will be attending the event. Perhaps go to their social media site and introduce yourself around.

"If you can connect in advance it won't be a cold start and if people are talking about the event on social media it shows they should be happy to meet people at the event itself", according to Stefan Thomas, introverted author of <u>Networking for Dummies</u>.

4. Clever Patois

There's no need for it. Thomas reassures that "people get really het up about finding something clever to say but I would ditch the elevator pitch and try not to overcomplicate things," Much as you dislike small talk, at least it won't strain your brain.

You should just lay back and watch the proceedings unfold. Let your natural calm exude gravitas. Liza Walter Nelson, a psychologist specialising in work psychology, advises, "Introverts also generally have a depth of interests which means they are often full of facts and knowledge. As long as they come prepared, and quell the nerves a little, this can absolutely be turned into an advantage."

5. Turn on Your Listening Ears

You actually don't have to do much work. People love to talk about themselves, so let them, advises author of <u>How to Stand Out: Proven Tactics for Getting Noticed</u> psychologist Rob Yeung. Your work is to, "Prepare a handful of open-ended questions that you can ask pretty much anyone you meet. Ask about their job and their interest in the event, for example."

6. Quality Over Quantity

Instead of working the whole room, you could opt to meet just a few people at the event. Aim for small groups who have welcoming body language. Yeung says, "Rather than networking, I sometimes say to clients I'm coaching that they should aim to engage in netfriending – chatting to people and trying to identify the one or two they genuinely like enough to consider possible friend material. If you can come away with just a few possible friends from an event, then the work benefits may flow naturally at a later date."

Introverted Salespeople!?

It sounds a little counter-intuitive – an introverted person in sales. The image of a salesperson is a fast-talking, extroverted charmer who could sell a fridge to an Eskimo. They love social interaction, talking and convincing, and they are generally thick-skinned - rejection is like water sliding off a duck's back.

This, however, was what worked when sales was a door-to-door affair, or over the phone. You only had the person's attention for a short span of time, so you had to make your pitch from the get-go, drive in the point and close the deal as quickly as you could. The sales formula then was:

Intruding - getting a foot in the door.
Pitching - convincing the customer of the product.
Persisting - until the deal is sealed.

The fact is that this formula doesn't work anymore. The extroverted salesperson is out-dated. Technological advancements mean that it's very hard to get a hold of someone if they don't want to be gotten a-hold of. Now, sales is predominantly done via remote channels.

Notwithstanding this, even in the traditional face-to-face sales scenario, customers are now turned off by the fast-talking, in-your-face pitching of traditional sales. Customers don't like being pushed or manipulated into doing something.

Research shows that the most effective sales technique nowadays looks like this:

Research - gaining an understanding of the customer.
Listening - gathering information on the customer's needs.
Reacting - adapting to the customer's needs.

Researching, listening and reacting are the introvert's fortes. To research, you have to read and analyse a lot of information before you even talk to a prospective customer. Listening requires patience, something introverts have since they operate on a more laid-back timeline. Listening also requires the listener to refrain from putting across his point until the time is right. A good listener is receptive to the thoughts of others and sensitive to unspoken cues like body language and the tone of voice. Reacting means allowing the customer to set the agenda and pace of the transaction.

In light of all this, introverts should be the ones to go forth and sell. As is said in sales talk, "We don't need hunters, just farmers."

Take Charge

Introverts can be great leaders if you take into account luminaries like Eleanor Roosevelt, Gandhi and CEO of Campbell's Soup Co., Douglas Conant. Research at Harvard Business School shows that introverted leaders may more effectively lead their teams, if their teams are go-getters. Since introverts are innately good listeners, they will listen to their team's suggestions and consider them carefully, singling out those that will be of greatest value. Cain says, "Introverts are really good, if they have a bunch of engaged employees, at letting those employees run with their ideas, cultivating those ideas. They're less focused on putting their own stamp on things and more on bringing out other people's strengths."

Surround yourself with a proactive team, and find your own way to motivate your team. Cain says, "They also tend to be very good at cultivating one-on-one alliances with the people they're leading and really listening to what their needs are, what their input is."

Once they know what makes their employees tick, they can then delegate appropriately.

In his own introverted way, Conant encouraged his team by pinpointing the big contributors and sending them authentic letters of thanks from his own desk. How can these powerful luminaries be in their own space, yet make the huge differences that they have?

➢ Cultivate a strong relationship with a few key people in your organisation. They will support you to achieve what you need to achieve.

➢ Take the lead when it's required. Your team will value your leadership if they are given a chance to do it on their own too.

➢ Speak up when you need to. When you choose your moment to weigh in with your thoughts, those thoughts will be more valued.

INTROVERT

➢ Develop a solid way to communicate, be it face-to-face, online or on paper.

➢ Pick key social events to attend, and make sure you stand out at them. Psych yourself to put your best foot forward, and make the effort to stay throughout.

➢ Treat changes like pushes forward, because they are inevitable. Anticipate them, prepare for them, and accept them gracefully.

➢ Be prepared to act when it is necessary to. Organise it so that you can act smart.

➢ Remember to recharge, but be sure to inform your key people that you're taking time out to recharge, not to run away. Give them a set time as to when you will start being available to them again.

CONCLUSION

We've seen how introverts can not only survive in a predominantly extroverted world but hold their own and thrive, becoming masters of their domains in their social life, home life, college and the workplace. We now understand that social exhaustion is avoidable and manageable if we are smart about it, and we have tips on how to harness aspects of our personality to our benefit and advantage.

Keep in mind that all the suggestions in each chapter of this book are inter-applicable and interchangeable, as they all aim to assist you in either overcoming your natural tendencies to shield yourself from over-stimulation and energy depletion or using your introverted nature to rise above the rest.

Take strength in the knowledge that there are many powerful and beloved introverts who lead us and inspire us in every field. Here are just a few of the names we all know and admire:

Mother Teresa

Barack Obama

Lady Gaga

Hillary Clinton

Michael Jordan

Emma Watson

Leonardo DiCaprio

J.K. Rowling

Al Gore

Bill Gates

Abraham Lincoln

Christina Aguilera

Steven Spielberg

Albert Einstein

Mahatma Gandhi

Harrison Ford

Elon Musk

Clint Eastwood

Mark Zuckerberg

Jay Z

Marilyn Monroe

Warren Buffet

Angelina Jolie

Also always keep in mind that whether you are introverted or extroverted, being strong and secure in yourself and having a big heart are 2 keys to true happiness in life. One addresses taking care of yourself, the other addresses taking care of everyone. No matter what, never aim to be something or someone else. Be yourself and just that. Remember what Chris Guillebeau, renowned introvert author and blogger, said, "You don't have to live your life the way other people expect you to." Remember that you can be the master of your own life, and its greatest creator.

9 781719 171472